bloodroot

Tracing the Untelling of Motherloss

OTHER BOOKS BY BETSY WARLAND:

What Holds Us Here (1998)
Two Women in a Birth, Daphne Marlatt co-author (1994)
The Bat Had Blue Eyes (1993)
Proper Deafinitions (1990)
Double Negative, Daphne Marlatt co-author (1988)
serpent (w)rite (1987)
open is broken (1984)
A Gathering Instinct (1981)

bloodroot

Tracing the Untelling of

Motherloss

by

BETSY WARLAND

SECOND STORY Press

Canadian Cataloguing in Publication Data

Warland, Betsy, 1946-
Bloodroot: tracing the untelling of motherloss

ISBN 1-896764-29-0

1. Warland, Betsy, 1946- . 2. Warland, Betsy, 1946- -Family.
3. Mothers and daughters. 4. Mothers – Death – Psychological aspects.
5. Grief. 6. Bereavement – Psychological aspects. 7. Loss (Psychology).
I. Title.

PS8595.A7745Z53 2000 C811'.54 C00-930171-2
PR9199.3.W364Z462 2000

Edited by Ann West

The literary quotations that appear in this book (pages 68, 129, 134) are excerpted from Hélène Cixous, *Three Steps on the Ladder of Writing* (New York: Columbia University Press, 1993). Word definitions and etymologies are from *The American Heritage Dictionary* (Boston: Houghton Mifflin Company, 1981).

Second Story Press gratefully acknowledges the assistance of the Ontario Arts Council and the Canada Council for the Arts for our publishing program. We acknowledge the financial support of the Government of Canada through the Book Publishing Industry Development Program (BPIDP) for our publishing activities.

Printed and bound in Canada

Published by
SECOND STORY PRESS
720 Bathurst Street, Suite 301
Toronto Canada M5S 2R4

for the memory of my mother —

a.k.a. Mildred, a.k.a. Billie, a.k.a. Buddy —

a complex woman

humming herself

she is losing her hold
the weight of her life too great
lightening her load, letting go of
her story, all that trying,
all that striving
                    sliding away from her now
she is sliding away from her now
lighter, lighter unwriting herself
loosing her lines, wiping the slate
our conversations drift in one ear
                                        & out the other
their repetitions seem to soothe her
it's the sound not the words
happy as I've ever known her
humming herself to her weightless death

Blank Spaces

As I write about my mother I untell her.

She is dead. Ever absent.

As her daughter my knowledge of her as a person is inevitably and necessarily limited. Throughout the years we lived in relation to one another, we were most comfortable in ourselves when absent from one another.

We were each other's blank space.

My mother's tolerance of me was enabled by a silent pact that I tell her very little about my life. This narrative traces the blank spaces of what we could not say, of what will never be known, of what will never be fulfilled.

In other words, this narrative is about abandoning disappointment; acquiescing to grace.

The Incomplete Story

My dad prepared for his death quietly. His was an internal, solitary process. He would sit in his avocado-green leather armchair with my mother's obsessive household activities orbiting around him. Sometimes he sat and watched television without the sound turned on. More often he simply sat and thought for hours.

I wonder what she thought of his calm. I suspect it unnerved her — she who was incapable of such stillness — that underneath her constant motion she knew what his stillness meant.

My mother's dying demanded much more from us. She needed our presence. In one respect, you might say she trusted us more. Certainly, by this inclusion, she taught us more.

"Demand" is not the word — *opened* herself.

When my brothers or I were visiting Mom and Dad, Dad would tell us some of his thoughts. There was the expected slow reviewing of his life, like a freight train reducing its speed on unstable tracks, but what moved me more were his spiritual shifts. Ambition no longer drove him. He had time now to notice insights springing up like brilliant wildflowers along the tracks.

As his formidable accomplishments faded from other people's minds, they faded from his. The self-made man now knew that what mattered wasn't how you had succeeded, but how you had loved.

I think my dad had decided to die quickly and at home. Illness had periodically hospitalized him over the years; this was not the environment in which he wanted to meet his death. A few days before he died, he asked his closest friend to "take care of" my mom.

A few evenings later he listened to the Christmas Eve choral singing on television. He had asked Mom to come sit with him: it was "so beautiful." She was preoccupied with baking a cake. As always, he went to bed before her. Then she heard him call out her name.

She knew by his tone something was wrong.

As she struggled to get him into his bed, he died.

Though there was the shock of Dad's sudden death, we had sensed it coming. We knew he was more than ready. Our mom, however, was not. She was unable to spend twenty-four hours on her own. Now I see how her needs overshadowed the grieving of our father's death. Yet, I also sense he didn't need our sadness. He needed us to rescue her.

In the eight-and-a-half years between our dad's death and our mom's dying, my brothers and I faced the imminent loss of our second parent differently. We were more ready to come to peace; more in touch with our own mortality.

As I grieve for my mother now, and the loss of our bloodroot, my father quietly comes to me in my dreams; makes simple gestures of comfort and reassurance.

Each of my parents' dying and death were idiosyncratic: my father's death did not prepare me for my mother's.

Some elderly widows "blossom" after grieving the death of their husbands. It's as if they finally trust themselves to be untrellised. Mom was not one of these — she wilted. Without the insular safety and familiarity of my father's presence, she was helpless. The only option which was viable for her was to move into the local nursing home where two of her siblings, an aunt, and numerous friends had also previously retreated.

My brothers and I, however, lived over a thousand miles away in opposite directions. We took turns "going back" to visit Mom every three or four months. One October, nearly eight years after Dad's death, it was my turn to visit Mom and her two "remaining" sisters. I always had travelled by air before but this time — because I wasn't living on the West Coast — I was closer and I drove. Midway there from Saskatchewan, while in Winnipeg for a friend's book launch, I was seized by extreme exhaustion. I had never been pulled down to this depth of weariness before.

The previous year-and-a-half had been the most chaotic of my life. Painful changes in my primary relationship had resulted in the loss of my home and the community in which I had lived for many years. Logic suggested that I was simply feeling the extent of my exhaustion now that life was calmer. But this explanation didn't equate with the intensity of my weariness.

Someone was dying.

It felt like it was me.

I left Winnipeg early. Drove.

Drove.

The nearer I came to my mom and aunts in Iowa, the more this vortex of death enveloped us all. Of my mother's four sisters, only two were still alive. By my mid-forties I realized this was the generation I had bonded with, not my own.

Just as suddenly as this overwhelming sensation of weariness had come, it left.

On the fourth day after my arrival, at four in the afternoon, I suddenly felt better. Clear. It was like a switch flicked on inside. And, I sensed who was leaving. This time it would be my mother.

On the surface, Mom seemed much the same and there was no cause for concern. It wasn't a concrete knowing, it was an intuitive recognition. The only tangible change was that her eyesight had seriously deteriorated. She was good at faking it in simple situations, but in more complex ones — like taking her on a drive to see the fall leaves — she became uncharacteristically withdrawn.

There was a correspondence between her increasing "eye trouble" and her diminishing connection with the outside world. One didn't cause the other; it was a synchronicity of senses.

When I flew back for her emergency hip surgery four months later, this process had accelerated.

Mom was blind.

Soon after Mom's hip surgery, my brothers and sister-in-law each came to watch over Mom for several days. Even though I spoke with them frequently after I left — following closely Mom's discharge from the hospital and her return to the nursing home — I still felt uneasy.

For comfort, I listened to Jan Garbarek and The Hilliard Ensemble's "Officium" every morning. I happened to hear it in a music store the day after I came home and was magnetized to it; recognized it to be the sacred soundscape in which I could hold the space I was in with my mother.

I would meditate for her, think of her throughout the day, but this music was where I could actually "hear" what was happening sometimes even before it was manifest.

When my brothers and sister-in-law all returned to their homes, it became more apparent that my only direct connection was the tenuous umbilical cord of the telephone. I spoke with the nursing home staff daily. They remained optimistic that her eating was gradually improving. Occasionally, I managed to telephone during a rare lull in their shift, and they would bring the telephone to my mother, place it in her hand, and tell her to talk to me. Mom's voice was frail; faintly cheerful, but she would quickly weaken, then not remember how to hang up, and let the receiver dangle while I would hear her bewildered voice implore: "I don't know what to do..."

Mom wasn't getting better. She only seemed to be getting more lost from living.

In the midst of one of these "Officium" mornings a voice suddenly interjected itself between the saxophonist's riffs. It was as if someone sat down next to me on a bus, turned his head and said quite matter-of-factly, "Prepare the way."

It was then that I gave myself to mourning. Not so much for the likelihood of my mother's approaching death, but more for the death of my mother's interest in living.

I could hardly bare to think that the one who had introduced me to the early enchantments of life was now so utterly disenchanted with them.

Life seduced her no more.

Before Mom had her hip surgery she was given a spinal block. Consequently, she was conscious when they brought her back to her room. After the orderlies and nurses had settled her into bed I greeted her. She seemed both drawn to and repelled by my voice – like a deep water fish to an intrusive bright light.

Her eyes were all pupil. Only a thin rim of their robin's egg blue remained.

I gently held her hand – she soon withdrew hers.

When a nurse checked on Mom, she hissed "Stay away from me."

Those days were spent in a strange limbo.

The medical system was in full tilt: recovery the only option on their charts. I knew, as I felt Mom also knew, that she wasn't going to recover. But she wasn't dying yet either.

She was in the in-between.

On the second day after her surgery Mom's agitation began to grow.

She would forget her IV, then pull it out. Consequently, the nurses insisted upon wrist "restraints." They tied Mom down. This added to her disorientation and agitation.

On the third day a nurse decided to feed my mother more assertively. I had declined the nurse's request that I feed Mom: Mom and I couldn't afford to be alienated from one another.

I stepped outside the door.

After listening to my mother's increasing desperation, I went back in and saw her rearing up – despite wrist restraints – shouting with rage "I know what you're doing – you're trying to kill me!"

My attempts to calm Mom down again by talking to her or touching her only added to her aggravation. I decided to sit down in a nearby chair and match my breath with her turbulent breathing.

Within a few minutes our breathing slowed and steadied.

But when a male attendant came in to check on her IV, Mom shot up off her bed: "Stay away from me! I know what you are! You're the worst kind of people!"

Gradually, our breathing once again fell into a calm rhythm. I still hadn't indicated to Mom that I was in the room with her as every interaction set her off. She needed to be left alone. After a while, I heard a sporadic, soft humming. I took this as a signal that she felt safe enough to acknowledge that I was sitting by her bed.

"What are you humming, Mom?" She began singing:

> "I'm forever blowing bubbles,
> pretty bubbles in the air.
> They fly so high,
> nearly reach the sky,
> then like my dreams they fade and die."

She had herself back again. Her light-hearted young woman self of the Roaring Twenties.

For the rest of the evening, interspersed between easeful periods of quiet and small, almost whispered conversation, Mom would happily sing this song and I'd join her. This simple song. Its words of fleeting optimism in the face of life's temporality so apt.

Mom was rehospitalized for uraemia a month after her hip surgery. I flew down immediately. I went straight to the hospital from my flight. She was sitting up, her wrists tied to the armchair. She looked utterly exhausted. I sat down and greeted her. Her reaction to my arrival was completely uncharacteristic. She barely responded.

She had no interest in talking.

She only had one desire: to be put back in bed.

We sat in silence.

I struggled with my feelings about seeing my mother tied down again, but this time — defeated.

Then she matter-of-factly said "It's almost the end now."

"I know Mom — that's why I'm here."

Traces of any remaining hope vanished for me that evening. Since her hip surgery five weeks prior, she had eaten very little and her kidneys were beginning to fail. She was in the early stages of uraemia. She had been hospitalized in order to receive an IV, which they couldn't administer in the nursing home.

The following day Mom was clearer; happy for my presence. She made no reference to her dying.

Over the next three weeks she vacillated between talking about dying and seeming to be utterly unaware of it, like it was the last thing on her mind. I decided to ride her wave of consciousness: take her cues; follow her lead.

For many years, my mother's memory had been erratic. It had often been suggested that she might be senile or have Alzheimer's disease. I had always experienced her as having a selective memory, an "inventive" mind, which fictionalized when need be, and utilized oblique metaphors to reveal her most inner thoughts. In an odd way, this had prepared me for feeling comfortable with how her mind now moved toward its death; had already revealed to me that our held-fast notion of the unified mind is fabrication.

Unhampered by convention, Mom's mind now freely contradicted itself, split off in fascinating associations, conveyed her needs with fewer and fewer words, and sometimes presented piercing perceptions which appeared to come out of nowhere.

She was close to total presence. As with a child, what was happening was what was. With her shifts and contradictions, she felt no angst about losing the crucial lifeline of logic that secured her identity.

One of the things her mind was consistent about was me. Every few days she would say: "I want you to stay with me all the way."

I began to do whatever I could to limit the contact between her and the hospital staff. When I was with her I closed the door. Untied her wrists. Took care of as many of her needs as I possibly could.

As her body steadily self-destructed, our communication occurred more and more from mind to mind.

This was fascinating.

It was also frightening.

Every now and then the disembodied voice (which I became accustomed to trusting) uttered another phrase of instruction that was surprisingly concrete and helpful.

In the years leading to my mother's death, when I was visiting Mom in the nursing home, I would often find her asleep – head thrown back – mouth open like the last gasp.

Void of words – abyss of the mouth – unnerving.

That specific language of the lips (not words). Its vocabulary of shapes idiosyncratic as our fingerprints.

How we watch one another's mouth unaware yet deeply attentive. Know before words form, sounds issue, what its shape will say.

How when we abandon words and the mouth holds one of its familiar gestures, our knowing is even more complete.

Mom's face.

After surgery.

How it emerged from the bottomless.

Mouth drawn.

Hair pressed back.

Eyes black holes of underworld vision — looking at the living with no nostalgia.

The impossibility of sustenance.

The mouth knows it is merely a conduit.

The truth?

I am a gasping mouth.

As my mother starved, I too became more & more unable to eat.

This morning, as I write, a woman sits at a cafe table next to me. She is eating an apple. The sound, the gesture — crude; violent.

I momentarily glare at the woman.

She immediately senses my distaste: attempts to bite & chew more quietly. Soon leaves.

I feel the sting of guilt.

My greed for words — as crude. As violent.

There are no words for where my mother went.

In preparation for funeral home viewing, the lips are stitched together. The mouth sewn shut.

The dead's lips indeed are sealed.

Not by them. By us.

Hole knows.

Is content with impermanence.

Contains all.

Holds nothing.

(her mouth empty as folded hands in prayer)

As she starved she became purer & purer.

Spiritually, she seemed infused by a soft light.

Medically, she was becoming more & more toxic; her body slowly poisoning itself.

As I lost my appetite I was being initiated into another realm — a disembodied, highly conscious realm; the way of my mother's leaving.

In her last days, my mother's face became her mother's face. Not an exact, but an essential, eerie likeness.

Her hair was now straight & grey — like her "Mama's."

Mom's life-long weekly visits to the beauty parlour no longer separated them.

As with her bedridden mother, our family gathered around our mother's bed. Unlike Mom's generation, we came from far greater distances. Distances of all kinds.

My mother used to say accusingly "My children moved as far away from me as they could." She herself had been the only daughter to stay on the farm, two kilometres across the section from her parents.

"Times are different," we'd assure her; most of the kids we grew up with had also moved to where jobs and lifestyles better suited them.

Yet, as always, my mom caught a glint of truth.

Truth inside out.

Or.

Truth cut in half reveals itself.

Our mother had an imaginative relationship to truth.

She didn't out & out lie, she rearranged a story's parts like someone moving furniture in a motel room. It was presentation: how it looked to others. This was the basis of how it then looked to her.

Truth cut in half reveals itself.

As her daughter, I hated the liberties she took. With her cut & paste editing she had little regard for others' feelings or sense of integrity. I couldn't, however, think of her as a liar.

I still can't. I thought of her as afraid; then, much later, I grew to think of her as a remarkable metaphorist.

When my marriage ended twenty years ago, she informed me that if I were to come home for visits, I was to act as though I was still contentedly married. For over two years I had to fabricate excuses as to why my husband hadn't come along with me.

Eight years prior, when my husband-to-be and I were in the midst of making our wedding plans, we asked our closest, mutual friend to be in our wedding party. Upon learning Gilbert was one of the groomsmen, my father exploded.

Gilbert was from Tanzania. His father was the secretary of the Lutheran church for their country. Despite the fact that my parents were strong advocates for their own Lutheran congregation's support of "African ministries," Gilbert was unacceptable: Gilbert was black.

My father's red-faced ultimatum.

There would be no wedding. They would have nothing to do with me ever again. His ultimatum was her ultimatum: comply. Or "...never be part of our family again."

We eventually rescinded. We were married without Gilbert in the wedding party. Our wedding felt like someone else's but I couldn't get the frightening intensity of my father's stop-sign face out of my mind. Despite my father's robustness I had caught a glimpse of his impending heart attack. I didn't want to be responsible for it.

A year and a half later, when my husband and I were living on the East Coast, I heard my father's voice calling me one morning. It was so real and strange that I looked at the clock for some kind of reassurance. Later, I found out that I had heard him calling me at the exact time his heart had given out.

Over the years I would occassionally test my parents' parameters hoping they weren't as extreme as I thought. When I sent them my first book of poems, Mom said she'd show it to her sisters *after* she'd removed the first twenty pages (about the demise of my marriage) with a razor blade.

When my brother argued against her editing and pointed out, "Your sisters *will notice*!" she abandoned her plan. Hid my book.

I never mentioned the publication of any of my books again.

In fact, after that, I never mentioned much about my life at all.

Mom was lying on her nursing home bed for a little rest while I sat in the chair beside her. This was to be her last October – the Fall preceding her fall off the doctor's examining table. We were having one of those gentle, murmuring conversations as if side-by-side, enveloped by blankets and the tender dark. Suddenly there was urgency in her voice.

"I have another daughter besides you."

"*Another* daughter?"

"Umm-humm."

"What's her name?"

"I can't remember..."

By now I had learned to stay on the course of Mom's relationship to truth. Her strategies were the same as always, but her intention was different now: more revelatory, less concealing. Yet this one threw me. I did a double-check.

"Is it Betsy?"

"No, no: that's *you.*"

"So you just can't remember her name?"

"No. It's a simple name..."

"When was she born?"

"Before you. She wasn't really mine. I didn't have her. She'd been abused and I took her in. Adopted her."

"How old was she?"

"Oh, I can't remember exactly. She was young."

"How long was she there before I was born?"

"Oh...a few years. I wish you could meet her."

"What's she like?"

"Well, she was pretty wild when she was young. I had quite a time with her until she settled down. She has a good record now."

"Where does she live?"

"Not too far away, but she only visits me once a year. I wish she would come now."

"Hmmm."

"I get so lonely for her sometimes. She's such a lovely girl. You'd really like each other! I wish you could meet her. She keeps to herself."

"I'd like to meet her."

"She never told us much about her life. I feel sorry about that now. I'd like to know more..."

Then my mom does something I rarely saw her do. She cries. A delicate crying of inconsolable regret.

"I'd like to have known more..."

I was abused. I never told my mother.

My Mom was abused. She never told me.

Never knew I knew.

But my mother who had "another daughter" knew.

Truth cut in half — reveals its self.

There was no other daughter.

By splitting me into two, Mom's subconscious ingeniously found a way to acknowledge her loss: to reunite us again.

I walked the halls while they operated on Mom's broken hip. As I passed several patients' rooms, I noticed visiting family or friends often sitting with them in a strange, enervating silence. They sat apart. Rarely looking at one another. Staring inexplicably up at a corner in the room.

When I returned to Mom's room, I looked up to see what was there. A television. Here, on their precarious edge, people watched television. As if this were intimacy. As if this was what was really happening.

Death   a hole we fear to be bottomless.

When Mom hadn't been preoccupied with doing church & community projects, or performing extended family and domestic duties, she filled the idling space with words. Travelling with her by car was an involuntary tuning into her mind. Occasionally, she would lapse into sleepy stillness but mostly she provided a running commentary on what she was reading in the paper, what she had just noticed out the window (and what that reminded her of), and what was the latest about so-and-so. All subjects issued forth without the imposition of an organizing hierarchy of significance.

I now think of this trait with fascination, even a hint of admiration.

Underneath was an instinct for insubordination: she often saw things differently. Our resolutely standardized Norwegian-Lutheran extended family and farm community forced her perceptions to gravitate toward the in-between-the-lines coded and intuitive asides. Later in life, when with family, seemingly paranoid comments punctuated Mom's monologues more and more.

You never knew which form her sensing would take.

As her only daughter, I learned that when she appeared to be talking aimlessly she might well be scheming *in sub rosa*: suddenly she would have you diving for the ground with an angry ambush of accusation.

Like my mother, I also sense things others don't or won't. I too have fingered the curving line between imagination, paranoia, and accurate intuition enough to know just how fine a line it is.

The fine and elegant lines of words.

We base our belief in our superiority as humans on our acquisition of complex language yet it is the source of much of our suffering.

Written language depends on oppositional spaces: black & white.

To exist, language must separate itself from what it seeks to articulate. In the process, it separates us.

We scrutinize one another through the eye of language. We're more interested in what's been left out than what's been put in for as language is inevitably incomplete, so is story.

The more I write out of my life, the more I encounter the impossibility of telling the truth.

The lived story is far more complex than the fabricated one. This is the seduction of fiction: its containability. The certainty of words black & white on the page. The comfort of no one else's version calling ours into question. That sad yet sweet satisfaction when "The End" used to appear on the last page.

I had assumed autobiography to be an inscribing of identity. Suspected it to be an amplification of ego. It is quite the opposite. With every word I write I am reminded of deficiency. Incompleteness.

Every word I select is at the expense of others.

Other words = other realities known & unknown to me.

Writing...the truth is equivalent to death, since we cannot tell the truth. It is in every way forbidden because it hurts everyone.

Although I have never imagined I could write the truth of another, I did believe I could of myself.

EVOKE = REVOKE

Mark my word: the truer my self-representation, the greater the relinquishment. With each successive line — from my first carefully chosen word to the last, to the first reader opening my book — the story of one's self irrevocably becomes the story of an/other.

The barely concealed disapproval, then irritable disinterest, in many of the staff when they realized my mother was not going to improve. Illness is to be met with aggression: killing bacteria, fighting depression, battling disease, the war on ________.

Sometimes, there was nothing to offer.

Her needs grew further and further beyond our reach.

One afternoon while she was suffering she pleaded "Oh comfort me!" My efforts to physically and emotionally soothe her had all been exhausted. I desperately wanted to but was confronted by the closing door of my human limitations.

She needed to know this.

We needed to admit we were nearing that place of uselessness to one another.

I leaned close to her ear and softly prayed for her, acknowledging that she couldn't find the comfort she most needed, in us anymore — it was only to be found "in Jesus." This was her faith; her spiritual refuge.

Her relief was palpable.

She thanked me.

Then fell asleep.

This was the beginning of our parting.

My mom was a red-head all her life. The combination of her red hair & robin's egg blue eyes was arresting.

I've become aware, in the last few years, that the colour of her hair & eyes constitutes the colours which are primary to me: semi-arid ground & rock of ochre red with its sky of unmitigated blue.

My instinctive travels to Ayers Rock, Canyon De Chelly, Zion Canyon, the Grand Canyon, the temple at Knossos, and the New Mexico foothills of the Sangre de Christo Mountains have repeatedly confirmed the power and sacredness of these colours.

The red & blue of my mother's face.

This first and foremost face —

our impossible estrangement.

Mother — the dreaded reader of my life.

Me, daughter — the dreaded reader of yours.

Our stories — the necessary skins that separated us.

The clinging to one's true colours.

Truth, ∂eru–, tree.

How like leaves we shed them in our parting.

Truth, ∂eru–, truce.

More and more we sat in the silence.

When I meditated, I frequently felt the inner motion of her leaving process, and responded with an accepting space for it within myself.

Her absorption of this was immediately apparent — like a direct infusion.

My first home

(she housed me in her body)

being dismantled before my eyes.

Homebody.

Few of our family homes remain. These homes — their characteristic smells, shapes, colours, sensations, sounds — beloved & distinct as the grandparents, parents, aunts & uncles who made them.

Walking in the door — that rare relief of coming back to homebodies deeply familiar. Much the same, though intervals between visits lengthen; though we increasingly change.

The deserted bedrooms. The personal effects: the predictably placed hand mirror & brush; the winning ribbon still on the wall.

Memory, mousa, mosaic, muse, museum of the one who knew that bed like a craving.

Though the personnel have left or died, carpets and curtains have faded, the funeral home homebody whispers its continuity as soon as you enter. We hesitate at its front door but the memory of all our close-eyed family members laid out in their best dress or suit leads us in like shoe prints painted on the floor.

Three weeks prior to Mom's death my brother and I visit this final homebody to prearrange her funeral. As we approached the exterior double-doors we were simultaneously struck with the same shock of awareness: the next death will no longer be a generation or two removed from us, it will be one of us.

To plan a funeral for someone not dead is an odd experience. But, then, it's an odd experience to plan it on the heels of their death, too. The last time was when my older brother and I made the arrangements for our father's funeral. Dad died of a stroke on Christmas Eve. This was one way to bring us all together again for Christmas (something we hadn't done for years).

There's a suspension of reality at the intersection where neither life nor death seem substantive, yet flowers must be chosen, clothes selected, hymns decided upon. It's a time of twilight perception; the half-light of the funeral home its mirror.

We didn't know how long Mom would live but we did know we didn't want the weight of arranging her funeral to fall on only one of us. We didn't know who would be there when she died. Also, her two remaining sisters (eighty-four & ninety-one years of age) had some dissatisfactions about their two deceased sisters' funerals: Peg's hair looked "awful" – it hadn't been dyed; Chic's dress was a dark colour which she never wore.

It was a lingering discomfort: their sisters hadn't looked like themselves. We could see it was important to consult them; involve them.

Mom's two sisters happily decided on what dress she should wear. It was the deep-aqua one she had worn for her and Dad's 50th anniversary.

A week earlier I had begun the process — had Mom's beautician come to the hospital to cut her hair. Even though this required precious energy on Mom's part, it seemed the thing to do. Her hair had grown uncharacteristically long and the feel of it on the back of her neck bothered her.

During this time I also filed her nails, knowing that this would be the last time. I wanted this to be a gesture of intimacy, love for the hands that I had known all my life, not a cosmetic procedure done by a stranger.

I phoned the beautician once again and arranged for her to curl & dye Mom's hair, after Mom died.

My brother and I selected a coffin of polished ash wood. It was of a colour not too dark for Mom, and of a size not so monumental that it would overwhelm her diminishing body.

Home, kei–, cemetery

The lineage of hands. Like her bedridden mother (stroke-deprived of everything but one arm & hand), my mother's hands, when all her other faculties had failed, were eloquent in her final days, their habitual gestures a lexical comfort.

Her hands remained faithful: fingered her wedding & anniversary rings; tugged & adjusted bedclothes; surveyed her body's changes quietly as a seismograph; and lovingly warmed our hands when we came in from the spring-chill.

Her hands her last hand hold.

Occasionally, their motion would subside, and she would intertwine her fingers over her chest. Fall asleep in somatic prayer.

Sometimes, when unaware of our presence, she would reach up and rhythmically grasp the air for several minutes; eyes focussed; face content.

My brother mentioned this to his Vietnamese lover, who recognized this gesture of the dying: "In Vietnam, we call it 'catching fireflies.' "

One day, while in hospital, Mom held up her hand — her index and middle finger tightly crossed: "I'm so grateful you're here. We're so close, we're just like one!"

"Yes. We are."

And we sat quiet with this hard-found tenderness so late to come; so remarkably vast.

Then Mom astonished me.

"You made that happen, didn't you?"

I recovered by making a joke.

"It takes two!"

She smiled her crooked smile.

"Yes, but you made it happen."

Who sets what in motion — often the question.

Sitting in my optometrist's waiting room a flash of rage quickens through me.

The receptionist has just called someone's name; showed them to an examining room; slid their file into the holder outside the door; assured them with sweet-brittleness "Dr. Robinson will be with you shortly."

All very efficient. A routine check-up. Nothing to worry about.

So it was with my mother. A routine examination. In the safe sterility of her doctor's office. Danger the last thing on her mind.

Upon completing her check-up, Mom somehow ends up on the floor in a fugitive fall from the examining table. Excruciating pain. A broken hip.

It's hard to make sense of what happened. Imagine the scene — an old, blind, and easily disoriented woman left alone in an examining room — waiting for a nurse to come and help her dress.

A day later, we are told that the doctor had not left Mom alone. The nurse was there and had only momentarily turned her back when Mom got up off the table and fell to the floor.

It was clearly the patient's fault. How can we ever know what happened? Our mother's mind — short on short-term memory — predictably recalled nothing.

I kept thinking that there would have been time for someone to turn around; that Mom didn't move that quickly; that she typically indicated her consternation or confusion.

It often seemed to me that my mother's doctor treated her with thinly veiled disinterest over the years. Perhaps then it's not questionable that during the two months of my mother's resulting hospitalizations, illness, and dying, we never saw him; that no sympathy or regrets for what happened to my mother were ever expressed. My brothers and I briefly discussed suing but there was the possibility that we were wrong.

Two days after her fall, when Mom's doctor was uncharacteristically struck hard with a flu virus, I found myself wishing sleepless nights on him.

Should anyone have left her alone, or, turned their back?

Like so many questions about my mother, these too will remain unanswered.

What happened, happened.

And for my mother, they were of no concern. What she needed was for us to be beside her with peaceful hearts.

A piece-full heart? Just as the mind is not a unified entity, neither is the heart.

Most of the time, when with my mother, I was tranquil.

But as soon as I stepped outside the door of her room, this was often lost in the confusion of negotiating with the nursing staff; screening visitors; sorting out the needs of various family members; cancelling & rearranging flights, work commitments, lodging; trying to stay in touch with my increasingly distant life via phone calls with my lover and friends; and preparing Mom's obituary and funeral.

Within her room, waiting was a calm I rested in.

Outside Mom's room the waiting became increasingly exhausting. We all lived great distances away, so the comforts and respites of our lives were unavailable to us.

The shadowy motel room, sterile hospital, then nursing home hot-breath rooms blurred into one airless cell.

Even the restaurants, which provided a rare break, became intolerably dreary.

By the last week I found food revolting.

I became aware of a primitive notion at work within me: if my mother dies, I die.

It was a tenacious notion which persisted long after my mother's death.

Does this go back to our visceral knowing in our mother's womb: if she doesn't exist — neither do we?

It wasn't out of loyalty to my mother that the taste of my own death became so real. There was no confusion about our mutual love equalling our mutual death.

As close as we became, her death was her own.

Mine will be mine.

What I know is that it has been an almost consuming internal wrestling match. Like a birthing. Into motherlessness.

Progressively we were faced with the impossiblity of knowing what was really going on.

Sometimes it seemed Mom wouldn't last the night.

At the same time, a nurse would off-handedly say "Oh, she'll be around for months."

Some of our family were aware of periods when Mom was suffering while others gratefully concluded it was so wonderful that she wasn't suffering at all.

We had, however, finally learned not to dispute one another's realities.

Our dear family friend who visited daily, confessed to us one afternoon "Oh, it's so good to come here where there's love – all the Olsons do is fight with one another." Mr. Olson, a local farmer, was dying in hospital. His family was in disarray about who knew the right thing to do.

In this profound uncertainty, fear of our own suffering and death can fester into enticingly concrete righteousness. Create feuds which linger long after a death.

Amidst all this, even the brief distraction of watching old movies on TV eventually became too demanding; listening to music — too overwhelming.

The ringing of the black phone in my motel room would blot the entire space like a runaway ink stain.

Toward the end, carrying on a simple conversation with anyone required enormous effort.

We were treading water with no shoreline in sight.

During the final weeks of Mom's life, her older sister Lyla was in bed with a fractured spine. She was debilitated with pain. Depressed. Hadn't had a bath for days. Wasn't eating.

Her son was doing what he could but she needed the care a daughter might give.

It seemed no happenstance that my aunt Lyla's health was rapidly deteriorating at the same time her sister, nine kilometres away, was dying.

They were the two sisters who had remained in the home territory, whose appearance was so similar people would frequently confuse them. Theirs was a close yet prickly relationship.

I think Lyla felt the pull of my mother going down; the inconceivability of being the only one of her generation left in the home territory.

I gave her baths, got her eating, and we began to enjoy one another's company as we had for so many years.

The twin-like sisters were untwining.

As I moved back and forth between them I encouraged one to grab on to her still vital life; the other — to let go.

Though we know better, we want to believe that we can protect the ones we love. This is part of the anger — when you realize just how tied your own hands are.

They wanted to cut a hole in Mom's stomach: keep her alive by feeding her through a permanent tube. This would be "less invasive."

My mother was beyond making such decisions.

It was up to us. My brothers and me. Our decision matched Mom's body's resolve.

Even so, I discovered a nurse the following day preparing to do the procedure.

I stopped her.

The nurses continued to get Mom up in a wheelchair and bring her to the dining room table. Occasionally, I managed to convince them to let her remain in bed and bring her a tray, but most often they pressed on.

Mom was far beyond eating.

She would sit there confused — calling out to please be put back in bed, crying with profound discomfort.

For the staff, their concerns were: insurance regulations — they "had to offer her food"; the possibility of developing bed sores; and "the doctor's orders."

For Mom this amounted to inexplicable, sadistic torture.

Like a violent scene in a movie, I closed my eyes and ears.

Walked out.

When Mom was released from the hospital the second time, we knew what was ahead.

Without the support of the IV and without a feeding tube in her stomach, she would die of starvation and uraemic poisoning. It was a matter of a few weeks. Yet the staff at the nursing home continued to insist Mom was gradually improving.

They worked with old people who were dying all the time, surely they knew. Most of them, most of the time, however, gave no indication that they did. I cannot say why. In part, I suspect that the standardized regulations and policies under which they operated blurred their instinctive perceptions. Or, that their false assurances were what most families wanted.

I pictured them bringing Mom a tray of food, or another cloyingly sweet Ensure supplement drink, along with some encouraging words.

I imagined that when she clearly declined — they would relent.

I could never have conceived of the assault set in motion when one person wills another to eat. The action of pushing spoonfuls of food into my mother's mouth resembled sexual aggression, yet this action of providing nourishment supposedly was one of indisputable goodness.

Am I being too hard on the staff? Some were gentle. Others were not.

One day I called it to a halt.

Told the head nurse not to have any food brought into my mother's room. She reluctantly agreed (it was Sunday and she was short of staff — this helped). Mom hadn't said anything but she was withdrawn and her movements were cautious. In my mind I heard her say "I just want to be left alone for awhile."

By early afternoon I became convinced that she was struggling with severe nausea. I knew her history with this, that she rarely experienced it, but when she did, she could spiral down into days of wretching. She hated it. I didn't want her to suffer this now. She would be left with no energy for what really mattered.

During our uninterrupted retreat from the staff routines it occurred to me that Mom must already be very uraemic. Nausea is one of its symptoms. I sensed if we could just make it through this day without the smell or pressure of food, the nausea might pass. I asked that they test Mom for a uraemic count.

By late afternoon Mom finally spoke. "It's been so good to have it quiet — I needed it to be quiet. I was feeling so sick to my stomach." That evening, when I said her good-night prayer, she was more comfortable.

The next morning the orders to make her eat were in full force once again. Her doctor had been contacted by phone and he told the staff to feed her "...as much as possible." No one seemed to be taking the likelihood of uraemia into account. I felt a bit crazy.

I phoned the doctor for the test results that afternoon. Mom's uraemic count was so high that it was "...remarkable she's still alive."

Is a mother never?

Lying in her satin-lined bed; her final blue dress; her hair dyed red one last time; I stare at the pale stillness of my mother's hands.

I had not imagined this.

Her stiff, sallow body, face — yes.

But not her hands folded motionless & flat — a dead bird's wings.

There is a silent disbursement after a family member dies: a passing on to others when one passes on.

This disbursement is unlike a Will with its carefully considered assignment of assets and possessions. This is about possession, singular. This is about memory migration, and like migration, it takes time. Most often cannot be observed. Remains essentially a mystery.

While waiting for the technician to adjust my new glasses, I glimpse the profile of my father in a set of mirrors. His determined jaw. His intent gaze. His mouth patient yet expecting efficiency.

This was not a resemblance. This was the reappearance of my father's profile. I was taken aback. Then smiled with delight.

Nine years later it's good to see him.

And so we embody our dead. Their most characteristic gestures, preferences, postures, signatures of speech & perceptions, possess us, take up residence in those of us who remain.

Leaf buds hug themselves. Are not convinced by the birds returning — their signature songs scoring the stunned air with lyric abandon.

An orange butterfly appears at my window. It's the colour my mother used to wear.

The butterfly's brilliance is astonishing after all these monochrome months.

A year ago I was in Iowa with my mother.

Now, for the first time in this tentatively emerging season, I sit on the front steps of my own home. Close my eyes. Listen. Feel my body hungrily soaking up the sun.

For the first time, I meet this season without a mother.

The faces of the women I've talked with about my mother and me; about their mothers and themselves. The expressions on these faces as they listen. Their anger, their despair, their fear. A facial vocabulary unlike any other.

If you could see these faces.

Whether or not a woman is close to her family; whether or not her mother is dead or alive; whether or not a woman is or is not fully realized in her life has scant bearing on her feelings for the one who bore her.

These faces. One after another. Form rows in my mind like the photographs of women gone missing; those wanted for crime.

Not these women, you think to yourself.

Yes, these. The missing. The criminals on-the-run from the all too often adversarial narrative plot of mothers & daughters.

These faces haunt me.

Or, perhaps,

I haunt them.

Now I see what so few mothers seem to see, not the masks of distrusting superficiality, nor the masks of judgmental self-protectiveness, no, not these shields of hurt. Now I see the faces of distraught love. Faces of daughters who lost their mothers though these were the very women who raised them.

These faces were my face, no longer my face.

During the last year of my mother's life I finally understood her still birth as a mother (who was still a mother). And, I laboured in earnest to relinquish my need that she open her heart to mothering me. I gave myself to birthing her.

It wasn't that she didn't provide for my basic needs as a child — she did. But the motherly instincts of nurturing, taking delight in, & enjoying the female companionship of her only daughter, remained outside her imagination.

There was, in truth, only one possibility between us.

It was up to me. Up to me to birth my mother into the accepting arms she so longed for the embrace of.

She had been waiting. A lifetime.

I had been waiting. A lifetime.

It was not me versus she, but we who needed mothering.

How to

was all that mattered.

As I watched over her, Mom often said with child-like happiness "You're my mother now!"

A mother must be birthed back into herself.

What we had both dreaded was precisely what we both needed.

This wasn't entanglement.

This was entrustment.

Everything ends with flowers.

One day an estranged in-law came by to visit Mom. I hadn't seen her in a number of years. She and my cousin had split up twice and she was said to be "the problem." I'd heard she was doing quite well as a realtor.

She had that veneer women often accumulate along with their success, their "making it" professionally in the business world. From wardrobe to makeup to hairdo, her presentation was stylish, even sexy, but the end result gave the unmistakable, and likely necessary, impression of armour.

Yet, she was the one who knew to bring Mom a rose.

When I held it to Mom's nostrils — she inhaled it with surprising pleasure. Each time she breathed in she would exclaim "Oh, that smells so wonderful!"

It was as if that fragrance contained her only remaining nostalgia for the pleasures which had sustained her, for all other sensual delights had been left behind, one by one, during the last years, weeks and days of her life.

The single, red-fragrant rose was perfect for her parting.

It was during these last days that my lover flew to Iowa to be with me. She would sit soundlessly in the corner of Mom's room, gently infusing her love with ours. Mom didn't know of her presence and I sometimes would nearly forget she was there. As Mom abandoned her body, her room became an energy field in which the delineation of bodies and egos occupying that space became less and less significant. There was a sense of holiness in her room which my lover also gave herself to.

A day or two after my lover came, my eldest brother and his wife arrived and told us to take the afternoon off. We hiked down into the woods along the river. This had been my most cherished world to retreat to as an adolescent. It was in the adjoining woods that my mother and her sisters had been taught the delights of nature by their most beloved grade school teacher, Miss Kenny.

The first spring flowers were in bloom. Those very flowers which gave me such joy as a young girl were giving me that very same joy again as I showed them now to my lover.

That evening I told Mom of their blooming and her voice lifted with delight. She asked me to name them. I responded:

"Springbeauty, Blue Violet, the Yellow Trout Lily, Trillium, Wild Ginger, and Bloodroot."

She drank in each name with wistful longing, then surprised me with the intensity of her response.

"Oh, I wish I could see them again."

...flowers lead...by their roots, to the core of the matter. They lead to where we are going: we need them as guides.

To blow a kiss...

To be *agape: in a state of wonder or amazement...with the mouth open.*

The flower blooms. The petals open...

Flowers the exquisite mouths of the unknown; the underworld. Their long, stemmy throats. Their phonetic roots. Each flower's distinct vocabulary of fragrance, colour, shape, tells us nothing. Which is everything.

Imagine the mouth sans words. Imagine the mouth's vocabulary being comprised of fragrances, colours, elegant shapes.

Blow: a mass of blossoms.

The flower below, the flower above, wide open with love.

a gape, agape

The magnanimity of flowers — how after a scorched-earth policy, flowers are among the first to risk return.

The stop sign of my father's face.

His rigid warning.

A flower; its stock and leaves; its seeds; its root: how one part can be edible, even healing, another part toxic.

The opening of my brother's suitcase. A flower in the wrong landscape.

Ten years before her death my mother searched for his journal. Found it tucked between his neatly folded clothes. Read it. Discovered he is gay.

Our parents' reaction — worse than we had feared.

My mother: "I'd rather you were a murderer. This is The One Sin the Lord will not forgive!"

The drapes were drawn as tightly as the mouth of a corpse.

With the tender fragrance of orange blossoms lacing the air I walked toward my parents' Arizona winter apartment two weeks later.

It looked like Mom and Dad hadn't emerged since the taxi had taken my brother to the airport.

It was as if they had quarantined themselves.

I was the first person they talked to. Prior to my coming I had discussed with my brothers whether or not I should tell them I'm also gay — their response was "No. It will kill them."

A year later, my dad asked me about my relationship with the woman I had lived with for several years. "So what about this relationship — is it a friendship, or what?"

I told him.

He accepted it. Said he didn't want to talk about it then, that he didn't need "any more tension right now."

Several months later he raised the subject again. And we began to talk quite comfortably.

He was making that slow turn into his death. He knew what mattered.

During my mother's interrogation of my brother she kept insisting "Who got you into this?" He kept replying "No one. This was who I've always really been."

Finally, my mother broke down. Confessed that she had been sexually abused as a child. With the exception of my father and her doctor, she had never told anyone: the shame of not being intact.

After the diary-reading-condemnation episode, my brother kept his distance from my parents. He visited them once a year in the company of his children, whose presence not only automatically excluded the topic, but also distracted their grandparents from further confrontation.

A few years later our dad died. Then my brother's kids grew up and constructed busy lives of their own. Eventually he was faced with the prospect of visiting Mom on his own. He was understandably reluctant. I encouraged him to go. Having nearly always visited my parents on my own, I was more aware of the fact that Mom was mellowing.

He went. The unexpected happened. Mom bragged about him for months after his visit! Her friends and the nursing home staff had all commented on how smartly he dressed; on how handsome and considerate he was; on how he was such a gentleman. Then, on the heels of these accolades, her voice would drop and she'd confide "He had a problem you know, but he's fine now..."

At first I didn't ask her what she was implying, but after a few times this hushed aside got the best of me: "Over what?" Her enthusiastic reply was a complete surprise.

"He had a drinking problem. But he's over it! Isn't that wonderful?"

Even now, our mother's inventiveness makes me smile. Her sleight of hand replacement provided a problem she could work with: solve.

Memory.

Everything we do, say, think, feel is memory-based.

Memory is highly selective, subjective, and partial, even metaphoric.

We fool ourselves into forgetting this.

We will fight to the death to keep our memories intact, our version pure and predominant.

When in defence of our lifestory, we will stop at nothing.

In the face of death we discover how little of it really matters.

Bloodroot – pushing its way up through the thick ground cover of my words; bearing its petals on the heels of winter. Daring the in-between.

Bloodroot – flower of my mother's childhood; my childhood. Its stunning white flower only increasing the shock of its umbilical-coloured stem which "bleeds" like a severed artery when cut or broken.

Bloodroot/bloodline. The lineage of matrilineal love.

When Mom died, I wasn't with her. I was half a continent & a country away, sitting in a waiting room, waiting for the results of my mammograms. There were five of us waiting – the same number as my birth family. One by one we were each called back for additional x-rays. The growing concern thickened the silence already among us in the pink room.

An elderly woman was the first to be called back into the dressing stall in which her clothes were hung – the technician reassuring her "everything looks OK." Then the next – a tense professional women, who was told to come back in six months...there was some concern about... the technician's voice dropped below audibility at this point.

Mom was dying; a nurse had phoned that morning, told me Mom's feet were turning black – a certain sign. Feet, our literal connection to this life. When the body knows life is leaving, the heart often ceases circulation to the feet. Then it is only a matter of hours.

Mom's spirit was withdrawing: I could feel it becoming weaker; fainter, all through the day.

I talked to my brothers. One had been in a holding pattern at his in-laws and was half-a-day away from Mom. I phoned her dear ones there: her sister; our closest family friends; Mom's pastor. They sat with her. And her favourite nurse, Gwen, was on duty. I sensed Mom's total focus on finding her way out of this life. I meditated and prayed for her throughout the day.

A third woman in the waiting room is called back in for yet another worrying round of x-rays.

Here we sit, strangers suddenly on the edge of believing whether we are living or dying. We witness one another's outcomes with growing fear & dissociation.

There is no intimacy in this room.

There is no small talk.

There is only the desire to get out unscathed. I begin to meditate for the other women. The fourth is called into her stall; is spoken to in hushed tones: the little I hear does not sound good. Finally my name is called out: the technician tells me to go immediately over to see my breast specialist and surgeon; she sends all my x-rays with me.

By the time I get back to my brother's apartment — surgery biopsy appointment in hand — my lover and brother are sitting quietly in his living room.

Mom is dead.

Within the first few minutes of conversation about my mom people often ask me with a strange sense of excitement "Were you there when she died?" It seems as if this is their only concept of death: that finite moment.

It wasn't that way with my mother. Death was all those weeks leading to that moment, all those days of distressing deterioration, struggle, small delights, and profound tranquility. Now I wonder if that finite moment isn't even death as we imagine it.

It is likely the most private moment of our lives; the most unshareable.

Moment, momentum, movement.

Movement, motive, commotion, emotion, remote, remove.

In the last two years of my mom's life, Gilbert (of my ill-fated wedding) "returned." He wasn't a "he"; wasn't "African" this time, but a Midwest-raised, soft-spoken black woman who was the most gentle of the nurses on Mom's floor. Gwen became the staff person to whom Mom most entrusted herself.

The extent of Mom's declining eyesight was difficult to track during her last two years. According to the optometrist, she had very little sight except for some peripheral vision and a small area two feet in front of her that was very blurred. Mom herself complicated matters by faking it, but even this became obvious during the last year. She never acknowledged she had grown blind. Maybe it was like a twilight slowly creeping in.

Whether or not she realized that her favourite nurse was a black woman is unclear. What Mom did recognize was that Gwen's care of her was infused with love.

When Gwen came on duty she would always shift Mom's increasingly stiff body to a more comfortable position; straighten her bedding; quietly ask Mom how she was feeling.

She would also consult with whomever of our family was there, which the other nurses never did. She seemed comfortable with, even happy for, our presence. She told us one night that it was unusual to have family gathering around at a time like this — most often they stayed away when their nursing home relative was dying.

Gwen's mother had died a couple of years earlier. They had been close. During her mom's illness, Gwen couldn't bear the thought of her mom dying alone: for weeks she came after work and slept in the chair by her mom's hospital bed. As the weeks passed, Gwen grew more and more exhausted. Finally the doctor insisted she get a decent night's sleep in her own bed at home. Reluctantly, she agreed.

Her mom died that night.

Gwen gave me this story.

It helped me to trust the necessary untwining of my mother's and my life when the time came for me to leave.

I had become exhausted through the two months of Mom's illness. My own life seemed distant and unreal in the face of her dying.

Other family members had reached their limits too. All the grandchildren had come and gone and my brothers, sister-in-law, and lover had either already flown back home or were departing in the next day or two.

I no longer had the stamina to be there alone. I knew that my own health was at risk.

We had begun to sense that what Mom had most needed – the gathering of all our love around her – was now an impediment to her letting go. It seemed that the little remaining energy she possessed was needed for the new life she was on the brink of meeting.

I booked my flight to Vancouver for the next day.

We'll never know if our perceptions were accurate. Did they just suit our own needs? Were they truly based on Mom's needs as well?

We didn't speak our final goodbye. Mom didn't repeat that she wanted me to stay with her "all the way." I didn't try to ameliorate or falsify our last goodbye by assuring her that I'd be back in a few days. We knew this was irrelevant.

"Mom, I have to leave early tomorrow morning. I've got some work I have to do, and a medical appointment I need to go back to Vancouver for."

No response.

Did she grasp what I just said?

Then she replied.

"Yes, you better go then."

We sat in silence, peacefully.

Then she took my hand.

This surprised me because she had abandoned touch a few days earlier. She held my hand beneath her cheek, so very tenderly. The contentment was so complete that I began to think she had fallen asleep again.

Slowly I became aware that this was not the contentment of sleep, it was similar, but much deeper. Then I noticed it, a current of pure love flowing from her arm and hand into mine. So light yet so strong, like a transfusion of energy pouring into me. Nothing else existed. Only this for ten, fifteen minutes. I felt so profoundly grateful. Blessed. But also a little frightened. What did this mean? Did this mean I too was dying? Or, was my mom passing on to me a way of living that she had only just begun to realize?

When she did fall asleep I thanked her. Kissed her smooth forehead. Looked at what little remained of her, for one last time.

Whispered "Goodbye, Mom."

To write this: our final goodbye.

Out of my body

onto page with sob and shake.

How we began — sustenance flowing from my mother through the umbilical cord to me — was how we ended: sustenance spiriting from her arm into mine.

All those years of alienation in between.

The faces of so many of the daughters who want to hear my story — their jaws locked with impossibility. Their mouths quivering with longing.

Mothers & daughters.

We have shared the same body in every sense:
this is why we fear one another, this is why.

The mothers are waiting.

As she became more and more trusting of what we call the unknown, Mom's life-long companion that gripped her hand so tightly, drifted away...

fear drifted away...

what remained stunned me.

The perfection of my mother's spirit stunned me.

As I walked out through the heavy glass and metal doors of the nursing home for the last time, the spring-soft light held me and I felt curiously weightless.

No, not weightlessness but no heavier nor lighter than anything surrounding me. Not on it, nor in it, but amidst it: earth my mother now. Not a concept, even a belief, but visceral.

My birth-mother had anointed me.

Not long after my father died my mother began to say to me "You're my *only* daughter!" She'd inevitably say this to me, nearing the end of my visit, in anticipation of my departure. Although she stated it as a complete sentence there was, in fact, an emotional dash lingering after "daughter": how could you leave me here alone; why don't you visit me more often; why don't you move back and take care of me?

Though given the option, Mom had declined living in a retirement home near one of us. We lived in unfamiliar territories. She wanted to remain where she had lived her entire life. My brothers and I understood her need to remain in her community. Our father often said "When I go somewhere else — I'm just an old man. At least here, people know who I am; what I've done with my life."

Underneath, Mom knew none of us could make a life for ourselves "back home." Also, like us, she felt the various long-standing tensions between herself & each of us tightening like a noose after four or five days together.

But, what we know, and what we long for, are rarely the same thing.

The necessity for separate territories took shape within me as soon as I was old enough to escape the house. The barn, the out buildings, the windbreak woods, the creek two kilometres away, and the river four kilometres away, were my true homes. Not until I was in my late thirties did I understand that my mother's lack of respect for my personal boundaries was an unconscious corollary to the hidden sexual abuse I suffered, and she suffered, as a child.

"You're my *only* daughter!"

One day a response came to me.

"And you're my *only* mother!"

At this — Mom laughed.

It was one of those simple yet profound shifts: suddenly we shared a gesture to express the irony of our relationship. From then on, Mom's statement & my reply became an affectionate joke we repeatedly enjoyed.

Several weeks after my mom's funeral the voice, which had guided me several times during her illness, spoke to me again. I was in a state of deep relaxation — in the midst of a Reike session — when it pronounced a name "outloud" to me.

The name was two words indicating a particular movement of a natural element. I'd never heard this name before. I felt instantly drawn to it. I knew it must be a sacred name: not to be spoken in public; to be shared with only a very few people. But, I was confused as to whom the name was for. A few minutes passed. Just as I was beginning to think how much I liked the name and that it must be for me, the voice spoke one last time:

"Your mother is no longer your mother."

I understood.

This was how I was to address her spirit. I should call her "Mom" only when referring to her in memory. To address her ongoing spirit this way was not appropriate, was even disrespectful.

Her new given-name so different in sound and meaning than the one I had known her by. Unlike the girdled "o" of Mom — its vowels danced with motion & light.

Standing on the bloodbank I wonder – when does the bloodstream stop? Is this what death is for?

When parents die – abandon blood vessel – they still circulate within our thousands of miles of arteries and veins.

We believe they die but perhaps it is we who finally die to them.

Blood type: blood never forgets, knows its script inside-out.

Blood pressure: to be free of its red-red weight.

Twenty months later, I am in the foothills of the Sangre de Cristo Mountains where miracles are known to happen. Now here, I realize I am in need of one. The soil is the ochre-red of all my sacred dreams; the sky an adoring blue. My mother's hair; my mother's eyes.

Though the blood bath of her fear is over, I flail in its wake.

Or, more truthfully, in the absence of her fear the presence of my own has welled up.

Sometimes, with the pure-intensity of this red & blue, an almost imperceptible green hue shimmers over everything.

Is this the tender-green miracle I need?

Mothers never die.

At least it seems that way.

Feeling profoundly discouraged. Panicked. I ask my lover to hold me. After a few minutes I sob "I miss my mother."

Seated next to an older woman in a restaurant, I noticed how she takes pleasure in her meal and glass of red wine; how at ease she is with herself. Though we each are contentedly dining alone, something draws us into conversation. Our talk quickly becomes one of those rare conversations between two strangers.

She asks what I am writing about. I describe this manuscript. She replies how wonderful and important it is that I am writing it, then suddenly her face turns inward. "I know what it's like. I lost my husband and only son on the same day. They were here at breakfast. Gone by lunch. A car accident. Sometimes it seems as if they're still here and it never happened; sometimes it seems so very long ago; some days I wonder if they ever existed; some days it feels as if it were yesterday."

My mother longed for her mother as she lay slowly dying: "I wish Mama were here." The tone of her voice unlike any other I'd ever heard her speak. The strange sensation of it. An eighty-six-year-old bed-ridden woman with child-like tears saying "I wish I could see Mama."

My mom, in fact, seldom was able to offer me such comfort yet, as my mother, she always embodied that possibility. And though we find comfort in other ways, with other people, she-our-mother will forever be the only one who held us fast, without pause, for nine months.

Hiking back into the Sangre de Cristo's foothills, I notice certain formations on either side of the arroyo that have been sculpted by wind and rain, and in their haunting contours, arresting shapes, I sense something of the holy in this slow-slow-slow encounter of the elements: art which will never be statically resolved, art which was never conceptualized.

The cheekbones of my mother as she starved to death.

A shape is meaningless except in relation to another.

All sculpture is additive or subtractive. Yet, to add is to take away from what was.

How we suffer loss.

How we shape, carve, chisel, model, cast, scrape, emboss, cut our way through life.

Write, from Germanic writan, to tear, scratch.

Loss, the sculptor of exquisite beauty.

It had been difficult to decide whether or not to read my poem "humming herself" at Mom's funeral. I had written it the Fall before her fall when I sensed death circling. It had prefigured her dying.

I didn't want to foreground myself. Yet, I also longed for Mom's funeral to be more personal than Dad's. His had been strangely generic.

Two days prior I knew.

I knew I should read it.

My deliberation had revealed to me that though my mother and I had spent most of our lives estranged from one another, my career as a writer was in part inspired by her. I wanted to honour her lineage to me.

Unlike most women of her generation, my mother creatively occupied public space. As a kid I had often experienced her speaking in public with her various church leadership roles. She also was involved in radio work for a number of years, contributing to a Christian women's program. And she frequently wrote and performed amusing commemorative poems for family anniversaries and special events.

Her violent reaction to my first book had obscured all this.

She had shown me the possibility but was unable to embrace it in me.

Over the years I have given hundreds of readings yet I felt shaky as I walked up to the pulpit. Short of breath. Dry throat. Unsure that my poem would mean anything to midwestern people.

Afterwards, when we took our places in the back of the funeral home limo for the drive out to the cemetery, my eldest brother was already seated in the passenger's seat next to the driver. My eldest brother – the one who has made a distinguished academic career in quantification.

Suddenly he turned around, grabbed my hand & sobbed:

"That was beautiful, Betsy. That was just beautiful."

Tears flinging hot from his eyes.

The family cemetery is adjacent to the family home farm. Five generations of farmers working that land. When my grandmother was buried, the cows lined up against the fence. She hadn't milked in years; in fact, these weren't dairy cows. They were her son's beef cattle. Nevertheless, they hung their heads silently over the wire fence near her grave in strange reverie.

A cheerful blue tent. A short row of stiff chairs and harsh-green astro turf. An open doorway dug into the earth. Though sunny now, it has rained and hailed during the past hour and a half of Mom's funeral, so we make our way slowly over the saturated ground.

A row of stiff chairs on the edge of...

My mom's four sisters, the two that remain...

My father used to say "The Hovey sisters think they'll never die." Now these two are stunned to find they only have the other to look at: a deeply familiar but wrong image in the mirror (eight decades of the five of them lined-up in photographs). They seem reluctant to sit on the stiff chairs by themselves; these chairs on the edge of eventuality. No one makes a gesture of accompanying them.

The minister is waiting. The chairs are empty. I take a deep breath and step forward. Sit between my mother's remaining sisters.

His voice begins.

I am named after my two grandmothers, my first name being my mother's mother's name, Betsy. It's an old-fashioned name. I can go for years at a time and never meet another Betsy or see my name in the media.

When my mom's funeral is over, and all its related activities are finished, my younger brother and I return to our motel room. We recline on our beds with numb depletion. Not ready for sleep. Unable to focus on anything.

Neither of us are television watchers. Nevertheless, we decide to turn on the TV for some "mindless distraction."

My brother has the remote. He stops at a narrative set during a lovely fall day. The scene switches to an aerial shot of a small group of people standing around — an open grave — the minister's voice begins "Dearly Beloved, we are gathered together to lay to rest Betsy...(my brother and I are paralysed with disbelief)...Betsy...may she rest in...."

Fighting the fear constricting my throat I rasp "Turn it off — turn it off!"

I read an article, a number of years ago, by a man who worked with the dying. He maintained that although we're terrified of dying, what would terrify us more would be if there was no death at all: we need to know there's an end; a way out.

One commonly agreed upon verity is, "The one thing that is certain in life is change." Change is, of course, the source of much of our anxiety, anger, and despair. Is this why we are so attracted to the concept of ends? Is this yet another futile attempt at containment: certitude? And what about the notion that everything changes so much, over time, that everything eventually is much the same?

For those who have "lost" a number of dear ones, there comes a point when consciousness tips, shifts, and you discover that your thoughts and dreams are populated by "the dead" more than "the living."

The thick, differentiating wall we've constructed to reassure ourselves, becomes thinner, thinner, until we see it's really semitransparent.

Recently, when talking on the phone to my mother's younger sister, Babe, she tells me: "I dreamed about Billie again last night. It was *so natural!* I had a real nice time with your mother last night. I can't remember what we did, but you know, I dream about my sisters almost every night — not about my own family — and we always have such a good time!"

Our story ourselves.

My mother birthed me & birthed story in me.

Exiting through her lower mouth, I entered language through her upper mouth.

She spoke words to me as soon as she held me.

Her placenta of words began to envelope me.

With the wrenching absence of her warm, melodious body, obligato opera of her organs, I needed the sounds of her words desperately.

With each word her lips drew toward me just as they did when she kissed me.

My mother taught me language, which is how to exist.

There is no story without mother.

Sitting on a stiff chair just outside her youngest daughter's hospital room, my grandma waits anxiously, day after day, for Grace to ask for her. She will not walk through that door until her daughter Grace asks for her.

Grace, my father's favourite sister. Grace, the one everyone always said I so resembled. Grace, "the black sheep." Grace, dying "a beautiful" but tragic death at thirty-five years of age. Grace, who glowed from a deathbed conversion, the "room full of light."

Grace, the estranged daughter.

Grace, who never did ask to see her mother.

Grace, whom I never met, my mother pregnant with me at the time.

"Oh Betsy, you're just like Grace!"

We come. We go.

Grandma Warland, the one adult I was close to.

With me — her youngest granddaughter — she found grace.

Sitting on the stiff pew next to Grandma Warland.

Another death. Her other daughter. Margaret, her "good" daughter; her loyal one.

Midway through the funeral, Grandma finally breaks down "I've buried both of my daughters. It's not right. It's not right. It *should be me*."

At fourteen, these life-sobering words make a deep impression on me. I vow that I will never do this to my mom. No matter what, I will not die before Mom dies. Nor will I accept the seemingly inevitable finality of our estrangement.

I have not had as serious a conviction about living now that I have realized these vows.

There's much I want to give, experience, learn, yet I find myself lacking the will of my adolescent fierce resolve.

What sustains me is more simple. Surprising. Like the sharp-sweet fragrance of juniper suddenly filling my nostrils as I walk the foothills of evening.

Story is survival

yet

the story is never the story.

That conflict is believed to be absolutely essential in the construction of narrative is no happenstance. This is not due to our short attention spans.

The origin of conflict in narrative? Narrator's mind versus Story's mind.

There are many pseudonyms for it: plot, character, point of view, dialogue.

Underneath we suspect story to be unruly; unreliable.

Yet our vigilant effort to control lifestory only separates & exhausts us.

I'm on the phone, talking with my aunt Lyla who has just turned ninety-three years old while visiting family in California.

It's January. Freezing rain, high winds, snow and bitter cold back at her home in Iowa. She says "I just got out of there in time."

I ask her how she celebrated her birthday, and in a moment's anticipation I imagine a description of a special family dinner. This is not her reply. Her voice shimmers "We saw the butterflies! Did you know they migrate through here? They took me to see them, the trees were covered with them...yes, the Monarchs...they were everywhere!"

Millions of thin, orange wings caressing the turning light.

My extended family — so deeply rooted in Northwest Iowa — has nearly vanished, as have all those ironic and humorous stories my aunts told about their growing-up years while we sat around the table after finishing dessert.

None of us can recall them now.

With the death of grandparents, parents, and the relocation of our subsequent generations, we find ourselves sorting though boxes of photographs, staring with bewilderment at the old ones.

We are a family forgetting ourselves.

Lifestory far more impersonal than we think.

The "tender-green miracle" I came to the Sangre de Christo foothills for — I see now is a simple miracle, as are all miracles, like the 180 degree turn of the pencil rotating between obliteration & creation. It is not difficult to do; it is difficult to believe:

Our story is not ourself.

We are too much on the outside of story, whether narcissistically taming it or selectively taking it in.

The miracle?

Whenever we free ourselves from our devices.

Whenever we be simply of story.

So, my story stops here.

I have filled this book with words about how my mother, in abandoning control of lifestory, realized a contentment I thought her incapable of.

Now, I abandon my story of her.

In the end there isn't an end but an easeful resignation flowers understand.